FAR AND WEE

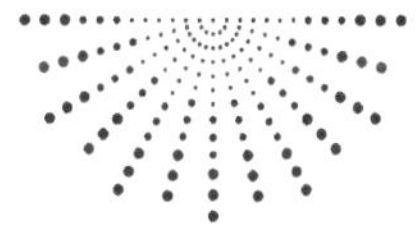

MICHELLE GARREN-FLYE

It's not possible that you knew, so it was just a coincidence.
Or a brief convergence of two universes.
Thank you, Balloon-man.

CONTENTS

INTRODUCTION

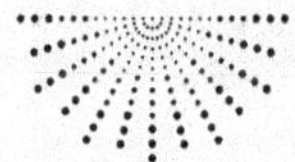

I first met the balloon-man in third grade. My teacher introduced us when I walked into my classroom and saw e.e. cummings's "[in Just-]" on the overhead projector.

That poem has stuck with me my whole life. The imagery of it is so sharp and clear. Splashing in mud puddles on days that are barely warm and still have an edge of chill. The colorless colorfulness of the promise of spring. It's childhood in a very strange package.

And then there's the balloon-man. Whistling far and wee…

I have no idea who the balloon-man was to cummings. But he's been in my life ever since reading that poem. He's inspiration. He's my muse. He's obsession.

I began writing these poems on May 21, 2022. I finished the illustrations for them on June 6, 2022. I've described this project as grabbing me by the throat and refusing to let go. I had to get it out. I stayed up far too late, but it didn't matter because sleep was unimportant. All that mattered while I worked on this project was finishing it.

That's the balloon-man.

It's June 7, 2022.

QUESTIONS

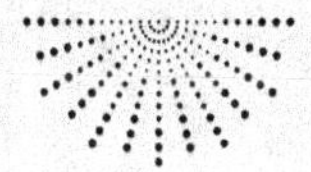

*I*n which we meet our heroine, who is waiting for something...

Balloon-man
Sonnet #1

How will i know the moment i meet you—
will it be heralded by ringing bells?
Proof of your love revealed in deepest blue
or a rosy pink as one of your tells?

When an angel crosses my path i think
probably should live a bit better:
give up the extra food and all the drink,
be a forgiver and a forgetter.

But when the light disappears down the road
my fallible human brain will deceive.
Promises in your presence i bellowed
are quickly hard for my heart to retrieve.

After all, the signs may not have been true:
you know, pink is just pink, blue only blue.

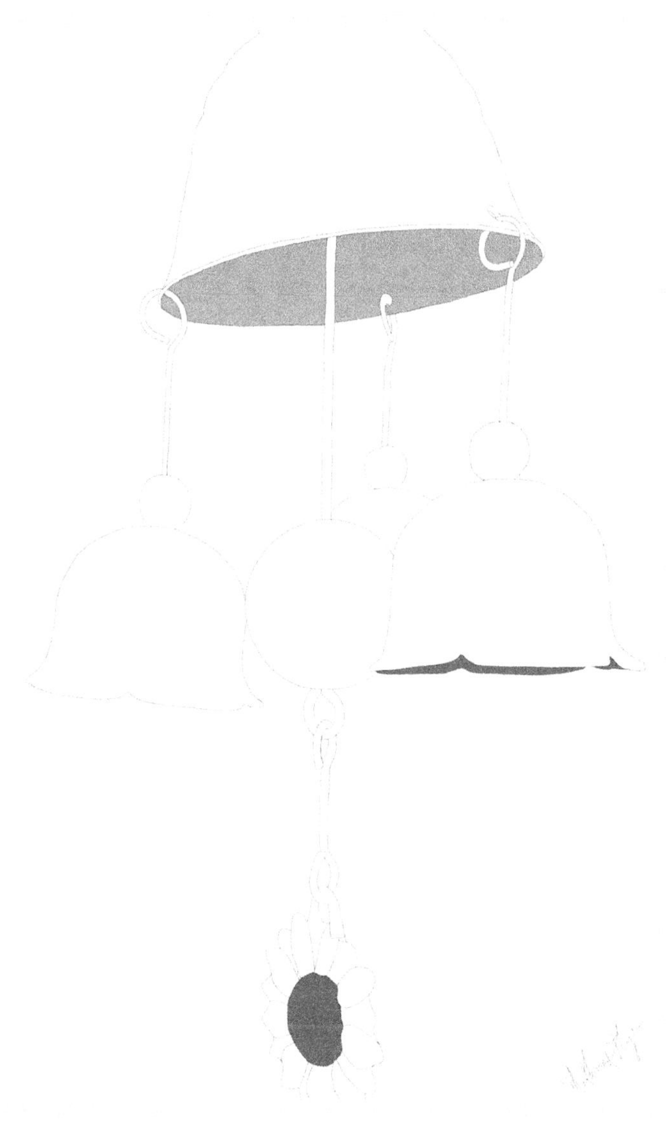

My Fall
Sonnet #2

Is that your whistle I hear down the road?
At any moment, you'll come round the bend.
I linger until it feels I'll explode
then decide it's better to call an end.

Waiting, after all, just doesn't agree
when my soul would rather jump into desire.
Balloon-man, can you just please set me free?
I'm longing to light my world on fire.

But you tempt me with orbs of pink and blue—
oh, lull me with eternal promises!—
You couldn't do this to me alone...true.
You know I know exactly what this is.

I willingly partake in my own fall.
I share the blame, the joy, the guilt, and all.

safe
sonnet #3

whistles aren't promises, or so you say,
far and wee or close at hand matters not.
i think you enjoy making me delay—
my life put on hold was always your plot.

balloons are nothing but captured hot air,
empty oaths clothed in thinnest of membrane,
secrets ready to burst out, best prepare!
in your hand, flimsy strings all that remain.

whistle far and wee, little balloon-man.
i'll wait no longer for your arrival!
maybe you've got a reasonable plan?
my future is mine, your only rival.

whistles can't promise, balloons won't provide.
my dreams will come true when i'm fortified!

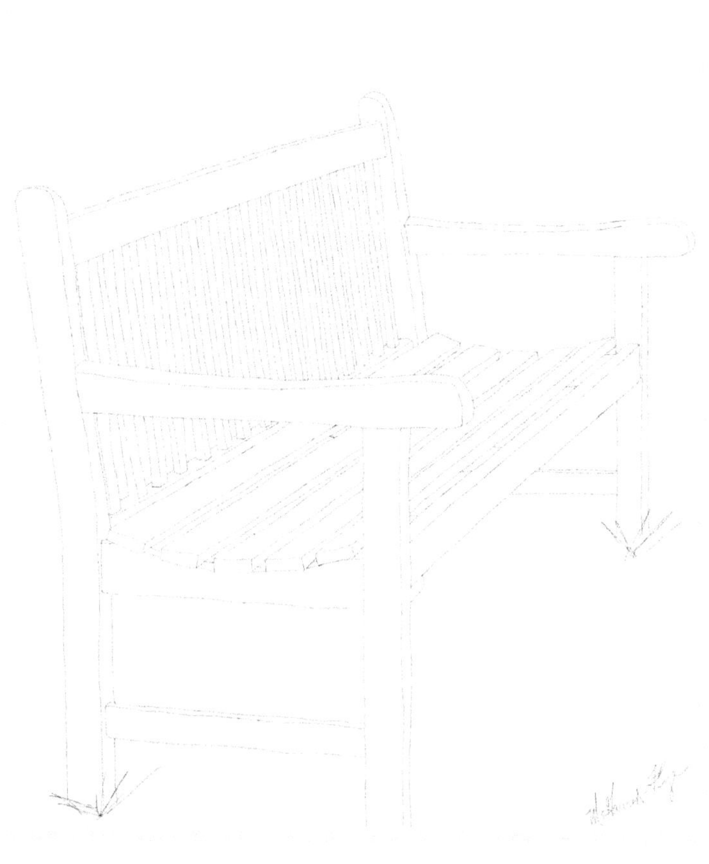

Who?
Sonnet #4

Who are you, I wonder, while I await
your arrival, my heart beating too fast.
Never met you, but I have known your fate
as long as I've known my very own past.

You've been there always, helping to inspire—
a muse, perhaps, in a very real way.
My heart is always yours to light on fire—
perhaps now you'll meet me, at least halfway?

In the end, my faith may yet be betrayed.
You may never be more than a shadow.
Just a whistle that tells me you're delayed—
a dream lost with the tears on my pillow.

I hear your voice—whisper soft in my ear
and faith will restore, my way will be clear.

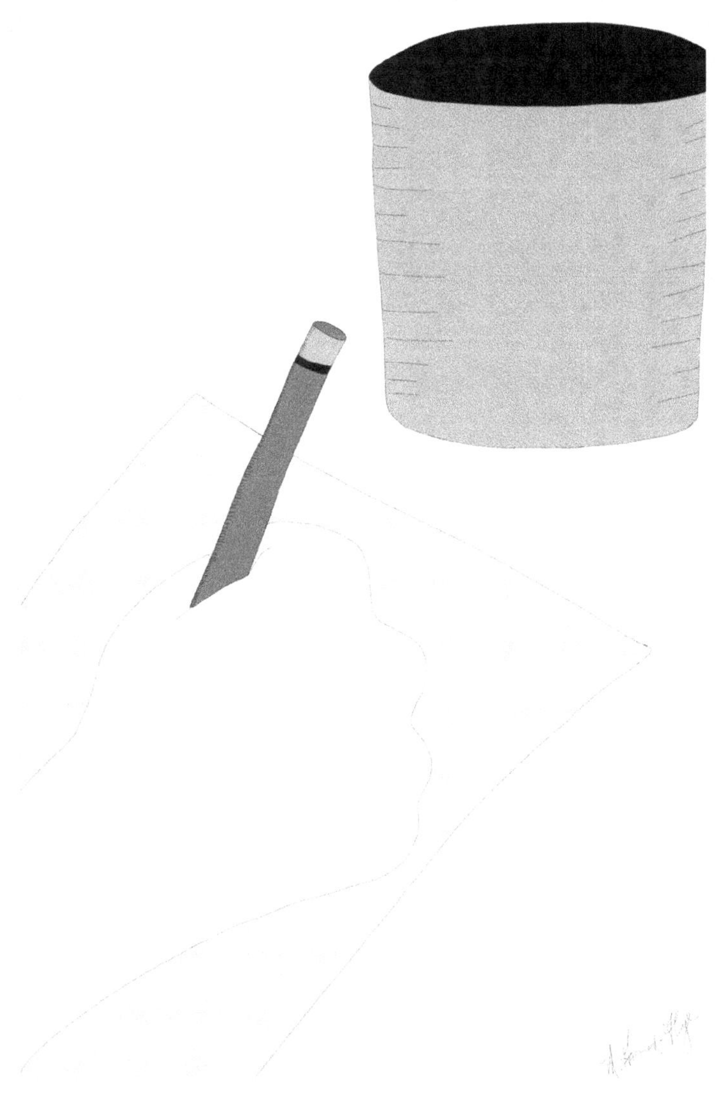

2

QUEST

*I*n which our heroine sets out to find the balloon-man…

Quest
Sonnet #5

What's the appeal of balloons, then, really?
They're useless as tools, not even good toys.
A light breeze will take them away, silly.
What's the use of balloons in all this noise?

Listen for my heartbeat, won't you, my love?
Let go the strings that restrain you from me.
I need you now, your whistle's not enough.
The call sets me on a quest, far and wee.

What dragons must I face to get to you?
I tremble in fear but know I will go.
What choice do I have if I'm to be true?
This is my last chance, I've just got to know.

No more waiting, time to make it all count.
Never mind the cost, I'll pay the amount.

Heart Compass
Sonnet #6

Shall I prepare now for it all to change?
For too long, I've waited, wished for your love.
Promise of a whistle at a great range
may in fact be impossible to prove.

What supplies do I take on such a trip?
Don't really know how far it will be,
only I hear you beyond skyline's dip—
Out among the stars where I cannot see.

Oh, whistle for me, you know I will come.
I'm following my heart, my compass bound.
The words you feed me, I devour each crumb,
there's no rebellion left, I come unwound.

It's your wish, I think, as I travel on,
your desire that I base my quest upon.

Doubts
Sonnet #7

Called to a quest—which direction to choose?
Follow my heart or a compass needle?
Either way, there is little left to lose—
a defeated return unspeakable.

Oh, but this journey is a lonely one.
I alone harken to your remote call.
So I set my face to follow the sun
and march along while my shadow grows tall.

Your mercurial self won't protect me.
Your whispers don't offer me much relief.
At each step I wonder if I should flee,
go home to my dreams—save myself the grief.

Hearts' desire is all that carries me now.
Ahead! Through the desert sands I must plow.

Heart's Blood
Sonnet #8

How do I stop wandering without art?
The paths I've taken I keep forgetting.
Stab the compass needle into my heart
in hopes of getting a better heading.

Of all our parts, heart's blood is the strongest.
My will returns, I know I can go on.
This part of the journey is the longest
as I bravely risk whatever's beyond.

I banish the voices that drown your song.
Listen with my bleeding heart for guidance.
Is this what you coveted all along?
Me stripped bare of all that gave me substance?

Naked and alone, I will stumble on.
Just faith left to base my action upon.

3

PARADISE

*I*n which our heroine finds paradise…

Peace
Sonnet #9

Your whistle wakes me from a sound slumber.
I let go the dream for reality.
So many days, they seem without number.
All for a chance to appease vanity.

Your trill leads me to a far distant shore.
Exhausted, I fall onto the warm sand—
I know I won't hear you here anymore.
Maybe it's time to find a place to land?

If so, there are worse places by far
than a tender coast with blue sea and sun.
Without your whistle I can hear a star—
it sings in last light when the day is done.

In the lap of waves, a type of release—
Is this the end in this feeling of peace?

Paradise
Sonnet #10

Paradise grows on me slowly at first
but clear sea and warm sand won't be denied.
Truly never knew I had this much thirst
for beauty in life I have occupied.

How is it that I require this much rest?
My life has been lived on a faster track—
I nurtured spirit and mind but not flesh.
In this graceful place, I find what I lack.

Balloon-man's call forgotten, I will play!
Make friends and dance with the wind and the waves—
why would I ever leave when I can stay?
Beyond love, this peace is what my soul craves.

Only at night when I gaze at the sky
and witness the stars do I breathe a sigh.

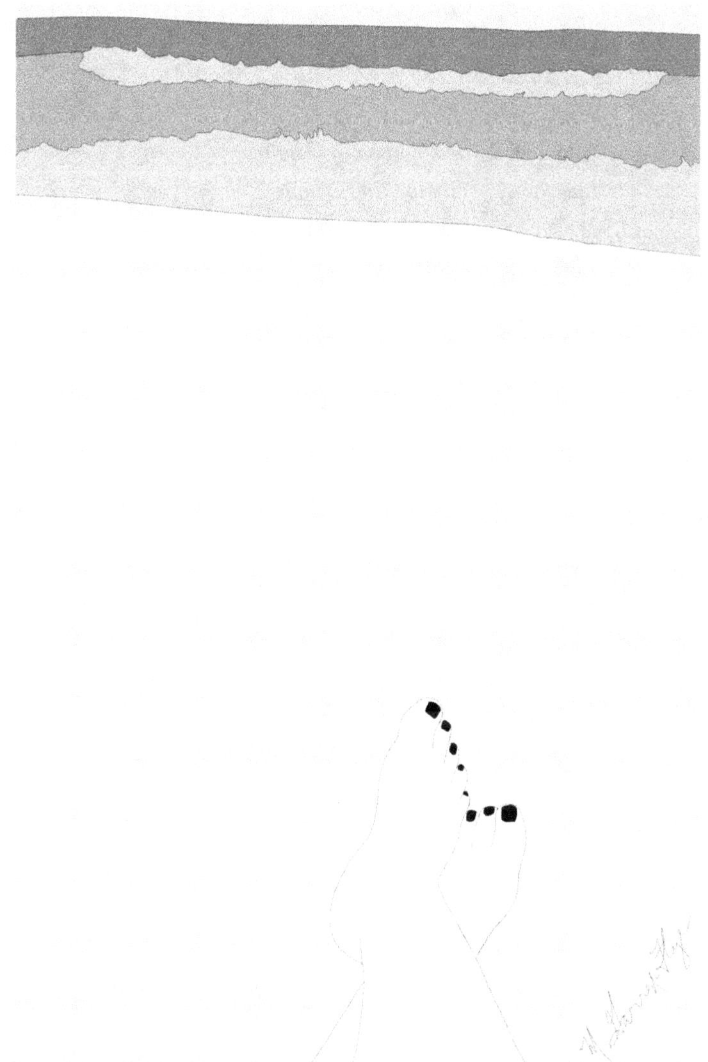

*Paradise Lost
Sonnet #11*

*How long have I lingered in fantasy?
I wash my sandy toes in surf, alone—
I can vaguely remember ecstasy
when you, my wayward muse, threw me a bone.*

*Closing my eyes, I cannot help thinking
of the days when your whistle would thrill me.
The nights I spent with your words tingling,
impatient for my pen to set them free.*

*And then I know paradise truly lost—
the sin of creativity emerges.
Warmth fades from the sun, leaving a deep frost
brought on by my own peculiar urges.*

*In the frozen silence that's left behind
I hear the call again for which I've pined.*

Forgetting
Sonnet #12

From the fall of paradise, I must flee—
from beauty and peace, now frozen in time.
My lost soul forgets, thinks of you only,
listens constantly for your words and rhyme.

Pen and paper alone may satisfy
this craving desire your call arouses.
Writing in the dark, I try to grasp why,
but reason breaks down as whim carouses.

Oh, back to my quest I know I must go—
face the dragons and monsters in my way.
I cannot afford to follow the flow!
No, I must leap headlong into the fray.

That's the only way to realize dreams—
by working until my heart bursts its seams.

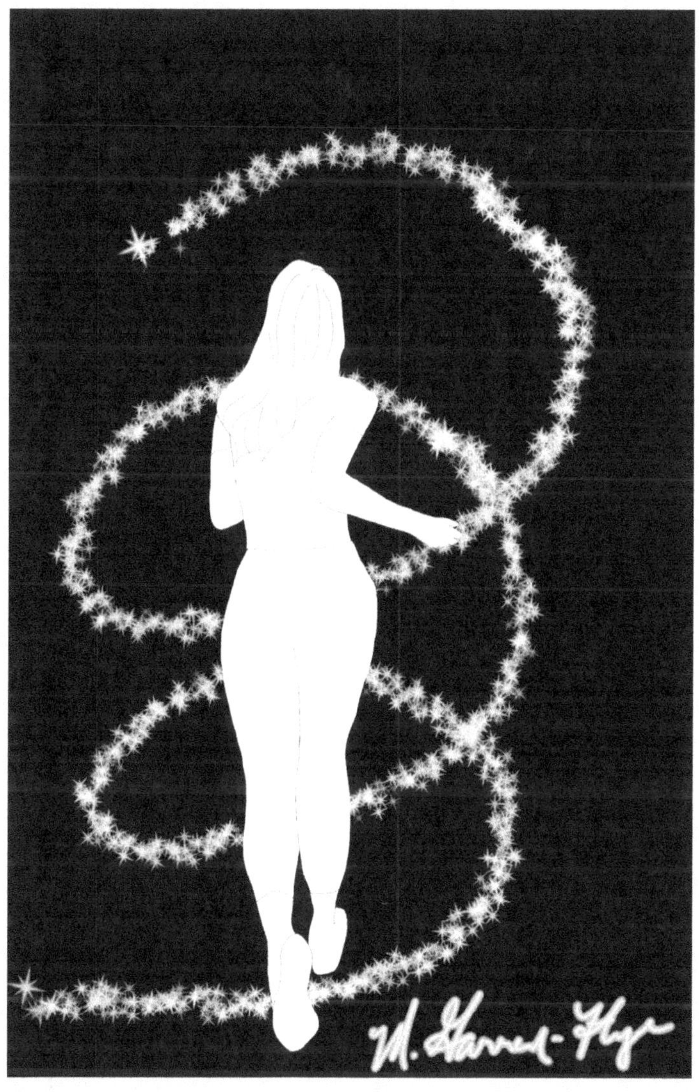

4
OBSTACLES

In which our heroine returns to her quest...

Faith/Doubt
Sonnet #13

Unlucky me, it's not you I find
when I round the bend in the yellow road.
What waits for me there is a beast unkind—
ugly and wizened, Doubt is his payload.

You will never find him, his eyes declare.
He runs from you, doesn't want you this way.
You think this life is going to treat you fair?
Love isn't something found just any day.

Though there's some truth in what he says, I know,
I refuse to succumb to his logic.
My heart's blood has spilled and from it will grow
a defense exceptionally magic.

Strength can be found in a Faith that is true,
and Faith in Love is a sincere virtue.

Fear/Belief
Sonnet #14

I've no sooner left monstrous Doubt behind
than my path is blocked by a lake of blood.
Miles away the distant shore I must find—
on the other side of this cursed flood.

Viscous and warm, the blood fills me with Fear,
of being alone and lonely for life—
How can I know this isn't my career?
Fear of my fate fills my heart up with strife.

But at my feet falls a large verdant leaf.
And I know exactly what I must do.
I step aboard, set sail on my Belief,
knowing I have Courage to be my crew.

Oh, Fear cannot breach Belief's sturdy hull.
My purpose is bright and will never dull.

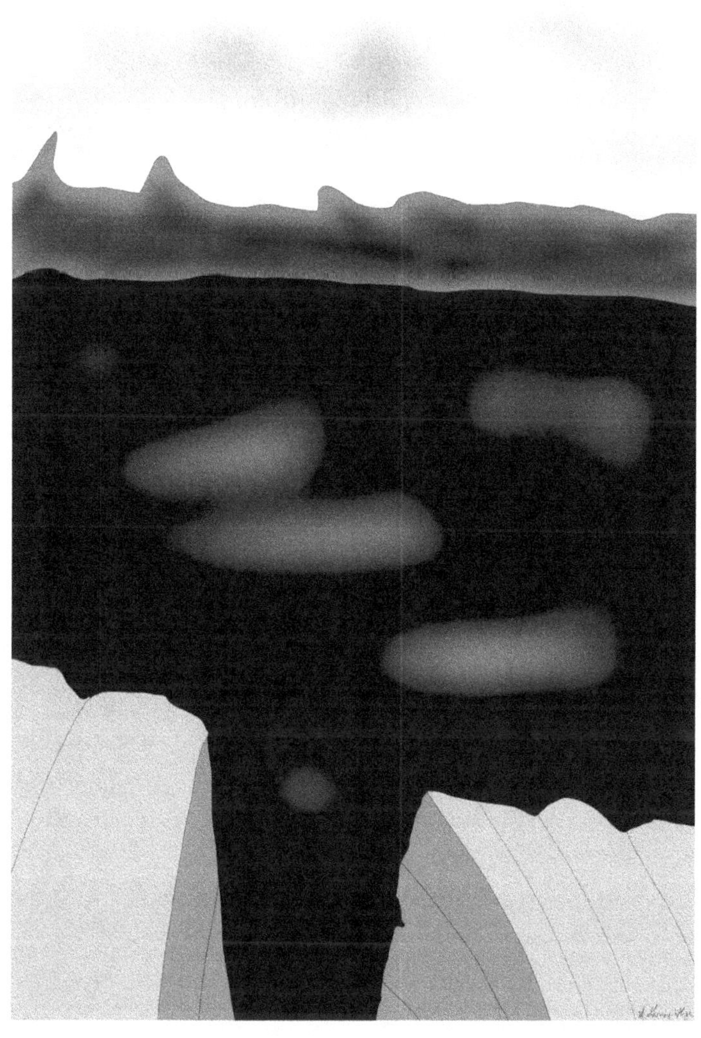

Adrift
Sonnet #15

Safe on my boat of Belief, I will drift,
alone still, listening for your far song;
crimson sea all around—what caused this rift?
What action could create a flood so wrong?

Blood laps at the side of my little boat—
I work hard to avoid each splash and drip.
Something made this sea on which I now float;
An event so awful it caused hardship.

Is it right I ignore what I evade—
what doesn't hit me will not hurt me—right?
My thoughts and prayers will come to the aid
of those visited by horrors each night.

In the end we are family in Pain
adrift on an ocean of bloody rain.

Discovery
Sonnet #16

Dare not sleep while relying on Belief
to keep all this fresh bloody Fear at bay.
Was this sea actually made of tears?
I can't help but wonder about the way.

Where is your wee whistle now, Balloon-man?
Am I left alone to fend for myself?
Darkness falls, isolating as it can,
I search inside my heart to find what's left.

What I find there surprises even me.
My courage never came from you; it's mine.
This knowledge was needed to set me free.
Even without your call, I will be fine.

Was it really you I set out to find?
Or a discovery of my own mind?

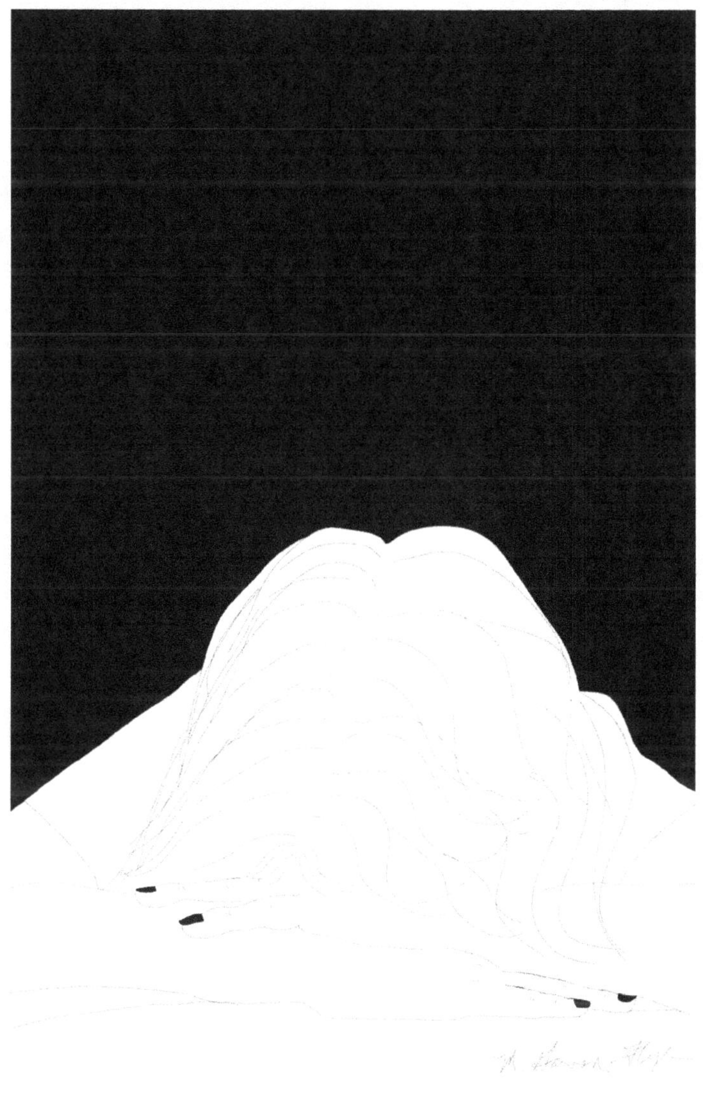

5

DAWN

*I*n which our heroine finds her way...

Complex
Sonnet #17

I gain the far shore with confident foot
and when I look back, I see only blue;
a pink dawn beyond my recent commute.
Perhaps that pattern itself is a clue?

Fear conquered holds no more horror for me.
Dread of what will come no longer haunts.
It's possibly okay to be lonely,
even while society issues taunts.

Lost in thought, your brief whistle surprises
and I turn without thought, know you are near.
Complex feeling within me arises.
Is it love, desire, or something less clear?

Only one sure way for me to find out.
I set off to find out what you're about.

At Last
Sonnet #18

Over a gentle hill, perched in the grass,
a mischievous grin, whistling a tune—
that's where I find you, waiting, at long last.
Behind you I see a single balloon.

Purple, I say, and shake my weary head.
What about all your talk of pink and blue?
Your fingers offer the balloon instead
of answering the question I asked you.

Silence falls after I accept your gift
and I sit beside you to watch sunset.
Being alone with you my spirits lift,
but lonely days without I can't forget.

Purple balloon bobs happily above—
just for a moment I bask in your love.

My Words
Sonnet #19

Morning arrives and I arise to leave.
Your fingers catch mine, your eyes do invite,
but I know to be me, I must believe
my future is mine, and now it is bright.

I take more from you than you meant to give,
so much more than just a purple balloon.
My heart may be lonely, but I can live
so long as the song I sing is my tune.

I'm sure in the night I will hear your call—
I won't resist, I'll even listen out.
Your whispers won't fade behind my wall
but they will no longer fill me with doubt.

Alone I am, but I hear my own words
take flight through the air, a flock of songbirds.

Home
Sonnet #20

Familiar surroundings greet me at home.
Here my coffee cup, there my own soft bed!
As if it all knew that though I might roam
I'd choose it, not adventure's call, instead.

Sleeping on my own pillow, peace fills me.
How could I ever have wanted for more?
I dream of you, true, but wake cheerfully.
My feet feel planted firmly on the floor.

Fantasy's design will always beckon—
I know my own wayward heart well enough.
Life will be full of musings, I reckon.
Dreams you and I share, but now I am tough.

I stand on my doorstep, content at last,
and hear your whistle as if from the past.

Michelle Garren-Flye stays up too late writing poetry and drawing. For some reason, she's never tired at 2 a.m., but when she's working at her bookstore the next day, she has to drink large cups of coffee. So far this method of madness seems to be working for her, though. Michelle is the happy mother of three incredible, mostly grown kids.

Far and wee is Michelle's fourth book of poetry, and she wasn't expecting it at all when she one day decided just for the heck of it to start writing sonnets. She's proud of this book. Unlike some things in her life, she doesn't think she'd change much about it. In that way, it's much like her children.

For actual information about Michelle and her writing, visit her blog: http://michellegflye.com.

facebook.com/michelle.g.flye
twitter.com/michellegflye
instagram.com/michellegflye

Also by Michelle Garren Flye

Poetry
Going for It
UnSong
100 Warm Days of Haiku
Hypercreativity: Poems
Far and wee

Sleight of Hand Series
Close Up Magic
Escape Magic
Island Magic
Movie Magic
Becoming Magic
Dickens Magic
Magic at Sea

Carolina Wine Country
Ducks in a Row
Saturday Love

Synchronicity Series
Strange Path: A Synchronicity Story
Out of Time
Time Being
Timeless

Set in the NC Mountains:
Weeds and Flowers
Tracks in the Sand

Published by Carina Press
Where the Heart Lies

Published by Lyrical Press
Secrets of the Lotus
Winter Solstice

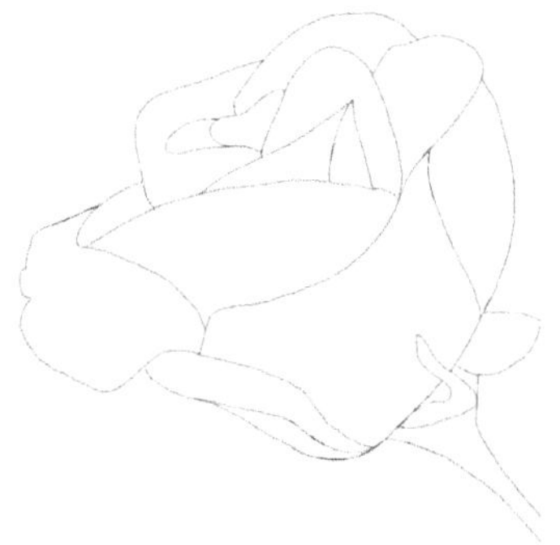

www.ingramcontent.com/pod-product-compliance
Lightning Source LLC
Chambersburg PA
CBHW071247130726
47998CB00003B/1084